church sound systems

by LONNIE PARK

ISBN 0-634-01782-9

HAL•LEONARD®
CORPORATION
7777 W. BLUEMOUND RD. P.O. BOX 13819 MILWAUKEE, WI 53213

Visit Hal Leonard Online at
www.halleonard.com

Preface: "Making Grapes"

So there I was in my grandmother's house, listening to records with a friend. Attempting to be sensitive to her musical tastes, we chose a modern rendition of an old hymn for our next selection. After the song had played, I asked her, "How do you like this version of 'Amazing Grace'?" She paused, appearing to be formulating her true assessment of the performance. Then she made her pronouncement: "What do you mean you're 'making grapes'?" We still get a good chuckle out of the story, but it brings to light one very important issue: If the listener does not hear correctly, the entire message gets lost or misunderstood. It is because of this fact that the sound system in your church may be the single most important fixture in the church. Let them hear and understand.

Over the years, I have worked with many and varied people who, probably like yourself, in some way, work with their church's sound system. Although church size and practice vary dramatically, all want the same end result: quality sound. They want the music and worship portion of the service to be pleasant for the congregation as well as the vocalists and musicians. They want everyone in the congregation to clearly hear and understand the message. Now all they need is someone that knows more than just enough to be dangerous: you. Rest assured, you will get all the attention you never wanted when the sound is bad. When the sound is good, no one will notice you, and you will be the silent hero.

Most available resources—often mistaken for sleep aids—assume that you already have a working knowledge in the field. They also go to great lengths to describe, in extended detail, the technical inner workings of every knob you may ever turn. That is not the goal of this book. The mission of this book is to introduce you to the basics of sound systems and provide you with the answers to the most asked questions. This will allow you to make your sound system work as efficiently as possible and even design the right system for your needs.

Sometimes it only takes a little information to become so much more effective.

TABLE OF CONTENTS

Introduction: Your Place In This World

A priest once said to me so sincerely, "You know, it is so important to us that people hear well." I replied, "That is, after all, why we are here." In order for you to be an effective sound person, you need to truly understand what it is that you are there to do. You are not merely the "waterboy"; you are an integral part of the team. Your job means much more than turning knobs and flipping switches.

Poor sound system management can stop the message from getting to the people. The people are in your church to worship and to hear that message. Any audio problems during your service will not only detract from the quality of sound but also distract or confuse the listener. You are the supporting link between the music or speaker, and the congregation. Musicians and vocalists set the tone for worship, the clergy deliver the message, and it is your job to get it all to the congregation in a pleasing manner.

In order for you to be successful in your endeavor, I highly recommend that you organize a meeting between yourself and anyone else who may directly interact with the sound system. This would include any choir or worship team as well as song leaders and clergy. Let them know that you are there to support them. This will help create a true sense of teamwork and allow anyone to discuss concerns and goals.

Find out what you can do to make them more comfortable during services. Can they hear okay? Are there any obvious problems? You'll be amazed at how this will help you get on the right track and start moving forward to better sound. You may not know how to fix these problems immediately, but assure them that you will get to work on them right away. Fear not, for with the information in this book, you shall be able to address most of their concerns. This will also get you on the road to a mutual understanding of your jobs and a better running team.

Part One: The Basics "Stuff You've Gotta Know"

Before we can help you improve or design your sound system, we'll need you to have a basic understanding of the parts of a sound system. There is some basic stuff that you've just gotta know. In this section, we will familiarize you with information and terms that most owner's manuals assume you already know.

Somehow, somewhere, someone decided that you, the operator of your church's sound system, are a well-versed audio specialist. Although some of you understand parts of your equipment's manuals, I would find it safe to say that most of you do not. That's okay. We will assume that you know very little about audio when we present the following information. For some of you this may be unnecessary, but you may find new and interesting tidbits anyway. Once you understand the basics, you will be able to derive all the information that you need from specification sheets and manuals. This will help you to spend less time staring at the manuals with that "first day in calculus class" look.

There are many variations and configurations of audio equipment. For the sake of efficiency, we will approach this using the most popular scenarios. Although every system is different, this book will give information that will relate to all systems.

Remember that the sound system can only be as strong as its weakest link.

chapter 1

Essential Parts of the Sound System

Microphones
(And Other Stuff You Plug In)

We begin with the fact that you have, or need, a sound system. This probably means that you need to amplify something (make it louder). Well, since you are in a church, you more than likely will have a person speaking, maybe even someone singing, and instruments, too. And I suppose they all need to be heard! Somehow, we've got to get the sound of that person's voice or instrument to go into the sound system and pop out the other end. But how?

Enter the microphone. Most of the world knows what a microphone is, or has at least seen one, so we'll proceed with that premise. The microphone is technically referred to as an **input transducer**. This simply means that it turns acoustic energy (sounds) into electric energy. In other words, it turns sound into electric stuff that can travel through a cable and into that hoojamajiggy (mixer) that you plug the mic into. We'll tell you all about that knobby hoojamajiggy soon.

There are tons and tons of brands and models of mics in this world. They all sound a little different and are designed for different types of jobs. Don't even think about weeding through this mind-twisting jungle until you've learned some of the basics. Also, don't buy the wrong mics or your whole system will be limited.

Scared yet? Let's make it easy for you. Without getting into every type of mic ever made, here's what you need to know. There are two common types of microphones that you are likely to run into: dynamic and condenser. Both have a thin membrane-like thingy inside them that vibrates when sound hits it, kind of like humming into wax paper over a comb (or am I the only kid that did that?). These membrane-type things are called **diaphragms**. These objects translate the sound into an electrical signal and send it on down the cable.

A **dynamic microphone** is probably the most common type of microphone used in live sound reinforcement. Dynamic microphones are very durable and less susceptible to damage by the the elements than other types, and stand up to abuse pretty well. They are naturally forgiving, and the technology is expanding. You will find designs available for almost every application, and these microphones can sound very good.

The second most popular mic that you will find is the **condenser microphone**. These generally are excellent sounding microphones and are better at picking up sound from a distance. The majority of your top-quality podium and choir mics are condensers. They typically sound very smooth and natural. Due to the nature of their design, they are more susceptible to damage. So don't drop them, play catch with them, or leave them out in the rain.

Microphones also require a power source in order to function. Many models have battery compartments. A more popular power source is the **phantom power supply** often built into the mixer. You can also buy a stand-alone phantom power supply if your mixer doesn't have that feature.

Other than a microphone's basic design type, every microphone has a pickup pattern. A pickup pattern, also called a **polar pattern**, is simply a way to describe the area around a microphone that is most sensitive to incoming sound. There are three popular types of pickup patterns. Since each miking application is different, it is really important to understand the differences when choosing the proper mic.

Chart of Pickup Patterns

Pattern	Picks up:	Typically good for:	Typically bad for:
Omni directional	All around.	Recording large areas, some lapel applications.	Everything else in sound reinforcement because they are very susceptible to feedback.
Cardioid (Unidirectional)	In a heart-shaped area in front of the mic.	Pulpit, choir, vocal, lapel, instruments. Good at general feedback rejection.	Picking up sound from behind.
Hypercardioid Supercardioid (Unidirectional)	Narrower area in front of mic and slightly from behind.	Pulpit, choir, vocal, lapel, instruments. Has good feedback rejection from the sides. Helps to isolate desired source by pointing mic directly at it.	Has poor feedback rejection from directly in the back, remember this when placing monitors.

Other Stuff You Plug In

There are some situations where you don't use a microphone to get the sound into a system. Sometimes, instruments and electronic devices have audio outputs. Electronic keyboards, tape decks, CD players, and electric/acoustic guitars are examples of sound sources with outputs that allow you to plug them into the sound system.

A **direct box** is a metal box with inputs for these types of sound sources, and mic-level outputs. Use a direct box when you want to plug these units into 3-pin XLR mic jacks.

Mixers

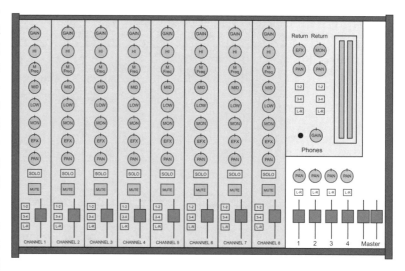

The **mixer** (a.k.a. that knobby hoojamajiggy) is the part of your sound system that all those things plug into. You plug all those mics, instruments, and decks into this unit and "mix" the sound together. You may hear mixers referred to as **mixing consoles**, **consoles**, **mixing boards**, and even **desks**.

The simplest types of mixers have a volume knob for each sound source that you plug in, and a master volume control. More sophisticated models give you many more controls and options. For example, some mixers not only give you a master volume control but also give you separate volume controls for subgroups.

And just what is a subgroup you ask? Well, **subgroups**, also called groups, buses, and subs, allow you to adjust groups of inputs. For instance, you could set it up so that all the vocal microphones are one group and all the instruments are another. In this way, you could control the volume of multiple inputs with one knob or slider (these sliders are commonly referred to as **faders**).

At first glance, these mixers can look like the cockpit of a jumbo jet. Knobs and faders everywhere, oh my! Don't panic, though; unlike the Rubik's cube, they design mixers to be solved. With a few tips, you will feel that cloud of intimidation and confusion lift away.

Look the mixer over, and you'll find the inputs and outputs; these are all the holes that you plug stuff into. On the face of the unit, you will also see all the knobs and faders. Each input and its own set of controls is called a **channel**. You can get mixers with four to forty-eight channels. If you have a twelve-channel mixer, you can plug in up to twelve sound sources.

As mentioned before, simple mixers may simply have a volume control for each channel. Other mixers have many adjustments that can be made on each channel. These controls are usually arranged as a vertical strip of knobs. If you can learn how just one channel works, then you'll pretty much understand the whole mixer. So ready or not, you're about to find out how that knobby hoojamajiggy works.

Controls you may find on a channel:

1. Gain/Trim Control – This control could be compared to a valve that delivers the proper amount of signal into the mixer. If there's too much pushed in, you will get distortion. If you don't let enough in, it will result in a weak signal and possibly noise (hiss and hum). The object of this game is to get as much signal as you can without clipping, which causes distortion. The gain settings throughout your system are called **gain structure**.

2. Equalization Knobs – These allow you to adjust the tone of each channel. Basic mixers give you bass and treble adjustments while more elaborate mixers give you multiple low, mid, and high controls. Some of these controls are even accompanied with another knob that allows you to sweep through and pick the frequencies that you are boosting or lowering.

A knob is not affecting the sound at the "0" setting (usually straight up). This setting is called **flat**. Turning the knob left or right will boost or lower the selected frequencies. Be careful, EQ-boosting can and will cause feedback (those annoying and painful squeals and howls you sometimes hear from sound systems).

3. Auxiliary Sends – Sometimes these are labeled **monitor sends**, **fold back**, or **effect sends**. These controls allow you to additionally send the signal from the channel out to other places like monitor systems, effect units, and recording devices. We'll discuss the benefits of these sends in more detail later.

4. Pan Knob – Typically this control is used in a stereo sound system and designates the mixer's output, left and/or right, that the sound comes out of. When you have a mixer with multiple subgroups, this knob is also used in those assignments.

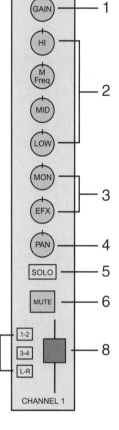

5. Solo Button – Usually monitored with headphones, this allows you to hear just the channels that have this button on. They're great for troubleshooting in the middle of services. To hear everything again, be sure to turn off the solo buttons after you're done using them.

6. Mute Button – Shuts that channel completely off. Many times, it has a light to show when the channel is muted.

7. Channel Assignment Buttons – Used on mixers with multiple subgroups, these buttons allow you to assign the channel to the subgroup(s) and/or the main outputs.

8. Volume Slider or Knob – Sets the individual channel volume. This signal is then sent to the master volume control or to its assigned subgroup.

The master section of your mixer is where overall adjustments are made. This section is usually located at the far right hand side. Just as you have controls for each individual channel, you have controls for overall adjustment. Here you will find the master controls for volume, auxiliary sends and returns, solo and headphone volumes and much more. These controls are kind of like the spray nozzle on a hose letting the sound out. If your mixer has subgroups, you will also find those controls here.

Okay, so here's the plumbing analogy:

1) You open the valve in the basement to let the water into the house (gain knob).

2) Then, the water runs through filters and water softeners to make it better (EQ section).

3) Now, some of the water goes to the water heater to be heated (effect send), and some water is piped off to the garden hose spicket (monitor send). Now the "betterized" hot and cold water flows to the kitchen sink where the faucet (main volume) controls the volume and mix of water flowing into the sink drain (master out).

Just like water, audio signals run out of somewhere and into somewhere else. The signal flows in one direction. This is why all those electronic units have inputs and outputs. The signal goes into the unit, is processed, and then sent out.

Amplifiers

The **power amplifier** is the "sound pump." It takes the audio signal and pumps it to the speakers. A mixer's output is not strong enough on its own to drive a speaker cabinet. By definition, an amplifier is an electronic device used to increase electrical signal strength. It does for an audio signal what spinach does for Popeye. It makes the signal strong enough to drive a speaker.

The more powerful the amplifier, the harder it can drive the speaker. An amplifiers rated output, measured in watts, is important to know. *If you have to push an amplifier to its limit in order to reach the desired volume, it will potentially blow your amplifier or the speakers.*

Amplifiers are typically packaged either mono or stereo. A **mono amp** is simply a device with one amplifier. A **stereo amp** has two channels, essentially two amplifiers, each with their own inputs and speaker outputs.

Some companies make units that combine a mixer and an amplifier. They are called **powered mixers**, **powered heads**, or **PA heads**. They are designed to make a more convenient product and are sometimes the best option for small and mid-sized systems.

Volume and electronic signals are measured in **decibels (dB)**, named after Alexander Graham Bell. The dB is very difficult thing to explain; in fact, I would have to say that even most professional sound people share only a limited understanding of it. Just remember that it is to sound what an inch is to distance, simply a way to measure.

Speakers

Speaker cabinets are the boxes that the sound comes out of. Every sound system has them. They vary in size, look, and design. Inside these speaker cabinets are various components. These components are called **output transducers** (things that turn electrical energy into acoustic energy, i.e. woofers, tweeters, and horns) and **crossovers** (the unit that splits the sound up by frequency and sends it to the proper transducer).

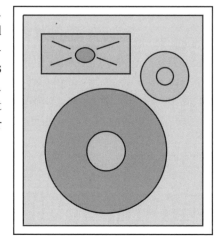

Transducers that you may encounter in a speaker cabinet:

 Woofer A speaker typically 8-18" (the biggest round one), designed to reproduce low (bass) frequencies. *Woof*!

 Mid Speaker This speaker handles the frequencies that fall between low (bass) and high (treble) frequencies. Although this speaker is not essential, some models utilize them in order to distribute the work so that each speaker can be more efficient. Many speaker cabinets that you will encounter do not utilize a midrange speaker. *Honk*!

 Tweeter Typically mounted above the woofer in the cabinet, this speaker reproduces the high (treble) frequencies. *Tweet*!

 Full Range These speakers are usually found alone in less expensive cabinets or mounted in ceilings and walls. Since they are responsible for reproducing all of the frequencies, they are not the most efficient option. They do serve well for low-volume utility jobs such as nursery or cry-room speakers where budget is more of a concern than fidelity. *All the barnyard sounds*!

Internal (Passive) Crossover:

Since the different transducers are designed to handle different groups of frequencies, something is needed to divide the sound up and send it to the proper transducer. That's what the **crossover** does. It sends the bass frequencies to the woofer, the highs to the tweeter, and so on. It is the component inside the cabinet that looks like a collection of electronic stuff in a clump with wires coming out. You don't need to know exactly how it works, just that it does. If you don't see one of these in your speaker cabinet, then you probably have a piezoelectric tweeter.

Piezoelectric tweeters have a funny name, but it's one you'll want to remember. They are fairly efficient for high frequency reproduction, but not for midrange frequencies. One benefit is that they are generally designed to act as their own crossover by filtering out everything except high frequencies. Since they are inexpensive to manufacture, and eliminate the necessity for a crossover, they help to keep the cost of the cabinet down. From the perspective of dispersion and fidelity, a tweeter using a **compression driver** (has a big ol' magnet on the back) is more popular but also more expensive.

chapter 2

Other Components You May Encounter

These are components that are not necessary for the basic function of your system but are used to enhance its performance. Technology has provided us with some useful tools that help solve problems and improve the overall quality of sound. Remember, tools are only as good as their users. A powerful cordless drill is a great tool unless you use it to pound nails. The following are some examples of these audio tools, some of which are also called **signal processors**.

Outboard (Active) Crossovers

We've already dicussed what a crossover does inside a speaker cabinet. As you will recall, it splits up the signal by frequency group and delivers it to the appropriate speaker. Sometimes, sound systems are designed using an external crossover, bypassing the one in the cabinet.

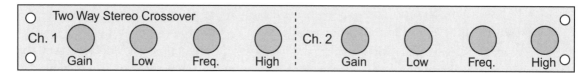

The internal crossover in a speaker cabinet does absorb some power from the amplifier, and therefore, the power is not being optimized. An external crossover splits up the signal by frequency before the signal is amplified. This process, called **biamping** (two frequency groups) or **triamping** (three frequency groups), uses a separate amplifier for each frequency group.

This practice is also useful when using a subwoofer. In this application, you use the crossover to split the signal between the subwoofer and the main speaker cabinets.

System Equalizers

Equalizers are used for two main reasons: to sweeten the sound, and to take out problem frequencies. The master system EQ (short for equalizer) should be used only to remove problem frequencies. On

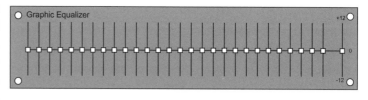

your mixer, you can use your individual channel EQ to sweeten the sound for each channel.

Small systems may give you a master bass and treble control as your master system EQ. Others use a graphic equalizer. A **graphic equalizer** looks like a group of skinny sliders with frequency numbers under each slider typically labeled from 20 Hz to 20 kHz. Use any master system EQ carefully since boosting frequencies can induce feedback problems.

Most system EQs are anywhere from 3- to 31- band. A **band** is a group of frequencies controlled by a slider. The slider typically has a center détente at its "0" setting. Moving the slider up boosts that frequency group, and moving it down reduces those frequencies.

These units, although similar to a home or car stereo, should not be set the same way. It is not wise to put any frequency sliders above the "0" point in a sound system application. The "0" point on the equalizer is the "**flat**" setting where it doesn't affect the sound. Later we will show you how to properly set the system EQ. Remember that you want to use this part of your system to remove problem frequencies and reduce feedback.

Compressors

A **compressor** is a device that is used to "squeeze" the sound. Since volumes of a given instrument or voice can vary so dramatically, a compressor is used to control the upper extremes. A compressor is a challenge to set properly and should be used as protection for your system in most cases. Set the compressor so that it stops the bursts of volume that occur from yelling or other speaker-blowing dangers. If set properly, it will allow your system to sound natural but protect it when needed. Compressors often have a built-in gate. Be careful, compressors can cause feedback.

Gates

A **gate** is used to automatically shut off the sound source plugged into it when the signal gets low (quiet). Gates can be used on individual microphones and instruments, or you can run the whole system through them. They help to get rid of unwanted sounds like hiss and hum, or background noises that show up when the inputted device is not active. They are electronic gateways through which the sound passes or is stopped depending on its strength. The threshold at which the gate opens and closes is user-adjustable. If set incorrectly, it will cause sounds to cut out when you don't want them to.

Room Delays

Room delays are helpful when multiple speakers are used at varying distances from the platform. It takes time for sound to travel from the stage to the congregation, and if you are using multiple speakers, this can cause a world of problems. If you are in the congregation in this scenario, you are hearing the sound from multiple sources. Yes, you are dominantly hearing the sound of the speaker closest to you, but you are also hearing the sound from the other speakers (not to mention the original voices and instruments). So what you have are multiple sound sources coming to you at different times resulting in a jumbled sound. The job of a room delay is to make the sound from all those sources hit you at the same time and therefore sound much more clear. In application, it "delays" the sound from coming through the speaker in the back of the room until the sound arrives from the other sources.

Recording and Playback Devices

These are most often cassette decks and CD players. They are used to play back music and record the services. Try to avoid using the same deck to record and play back since it is one of the leading causes of feedback and system-blowing activity.

"Split track" accompaniment CDs and tapes typically use the left track for music and the right for vocal. You can turn off the vocal track for performances or bring it in slightly to thicken the sound.

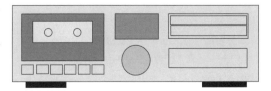

Monitor Systems

Monitor systems help vocalists and musicians to hear themselves and anything else that they need to hear. As any musician will tell you, this is a vital element of a quality performance. The most popular types of monitors are **floor monitors** (speakers designed to sit on the floor, also called floor wedges) and **hot spots** (small monitors that are often stand-mounted). These monitors are usually powered by a separate power amplifier from the main system (also called "front of house" or "front-end").

A good monitor mix makes musicians and vocalists more comfortable since they can better hear their performance. Some systems allow you to have multiple monitor mixes so that you can offer a separate mix for each different group of monitors. Although you'll need a separate amp for each mix, it is usually worth it.

A useful example is that a vocal group will want more vocals coming through their monitors than the musicians. You accomplish the different mixes by using the monitor or aux outputs on your mixer. To send a channel's sound into the monitors, simply turn up the monitor knob on that channel until it reaches the desired volume.

When hooking up the monitors to the amplifier, check the specs to find out the minimum load. Usually this is written right by the speaker outputs on the amp. It will say something to the effect of "4 ohms min." If it says 4 ohms min., then don't connect more than two 8 ohm monitors to that channel of the amplifier. If it says 2 ohm min., then you can hook up to four monitors. *(See the section on speaker chains on p. 30.)*

Wireless Microphones

Wireless microphones offer freedom of movement that corded mics cannot. There are many different models available on the market, and the spectrum is wide, but this is one area that you truly get what you pay for. There is no worse result than a message lost due to the poor quality or reception of a wireless microphone. There is a common misperception that wireless mics are better. Wireless microphones do not improve the quality of sound, just the freedom of movement. The explanations in the following paragraphs will help you understand what you are buying.

A wireless system consists of a mic, transmitter, and receiver. **Transmitters** come in the form of a belt-pack to which the mics attach, or for handheld models, the transmitter is built into the mic casing. The **receiver** is the unit with the antenna(e) that plug(s) into the sound system.

Wireless systems are available in either the **VHF** or **UHF** frequency ranges. There is less "traffic" in the UHF frequency range, and so it is less likely to experience outside interference. UHF systems perform best in "line of sight" situations where there are no obstacles between the transmitter and receiver. Although VHF systems are more susceptible to outside interference, they are more forgiving when the transmitter and receiver are separated by objects such as walls, racks, or a standing congregation. Surprisingly the actual sound quality is not significantly different between VHF or UHF, just the price.

Wireless systems are also available as **diversity** or **nondiversity**. A true diversity wireless system actually has two receivers, each with their own antenna. The system will actually switch between receivers to get the strongest signal. This helps reduce the incidence of noise and dropouts. A nondiversity system has only one receiver and is the more affordable option.

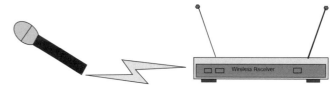

Assistive Listening Systems for the Hearing Impaired

For those who are hard of hearing, the sound system is sometimes not enough. Assistive listening systems allow individuals to sit in the congregation with a receiver and an ear bud (headphone-type gadget). The transmitter broadcasts the signal from the sound system, and the users have their own volume control for their own personal receiver. This can be the necessary solution for people who seem to struggle to hear even when the system is performing beautifully.

Cable Snakes

A cable snake looks like a garden hose with a box at one end and a bunch of cables at the other end. It allows you to plug in all of your microphones and instruments into the box end, which is set on or near the platform area. The other end of the snake is plugged into the mixer. It saves a lot of cable mess. The snake may also have **returns**, usually two or four jacks, that are used to connect the outputs of your mixer to the inputs of the power amplifier(s). This comes in really handy when your amplifiers are near the platform area and your mixer is quite far away.

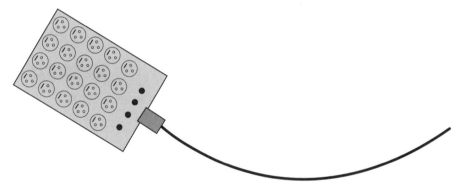

chapter 3

Connectors and Wires; How They Work

Miles and piles of cables are a twisting tangling web of regrettable necessity. Unfortunately, in order to hook all this stuff up we need cables, and lots of them. You will need to know the different types so that you don't make simple mistakes that bring on problems. Take my word for it, it is a lot easier to get it right the first time rather than to try to fish through the cable spaghetti later to find the problems. If you hear radio stations, strange squealing, hum, or nothing at all, chances are good that you may have bad wiring or just plain wrong choice of cable.

Cables

Speaker Cable

Connects speakers to an amplifier or to other speakers.

Speaker cable has two coated wires and no shield. Sometimes the cable comes in the form of zip cable (lamp cord type), but usually it's two coated wires inside a rubber jacket.

Microphone Cable

Used for microphones and as balanced patch cables.

Microphone cables have two coated wires and a shield. This type of cable can be run long distances without significant signal loss or interference.

Unbalanced Patch/Instrument Cable

Used to connect audio equipment as well as instruments.

These cables have one conductor and a shield. They are not to be confused with speaker cables; the shield plays an important role.

Common Connectors

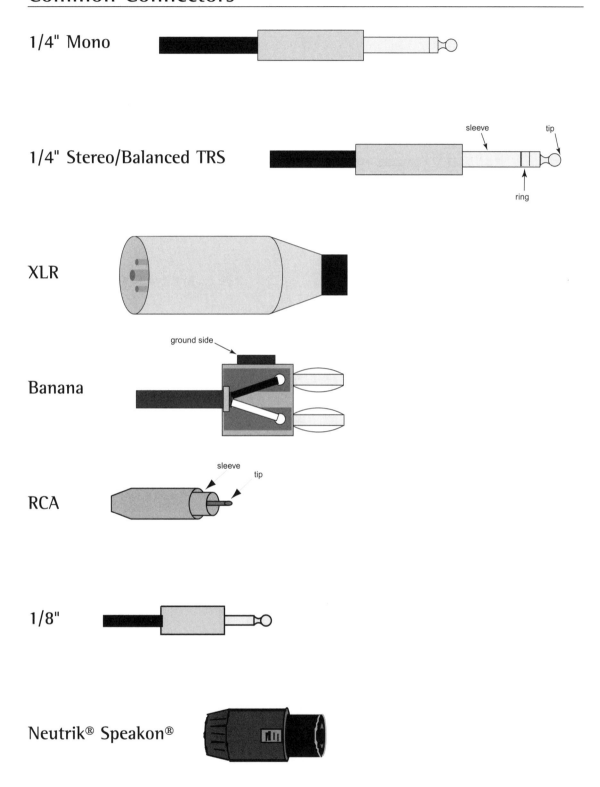

1/4" Mono

1/4" Stereo/Balanced TRS

sleeve

tip

ring

XLR

ground side

Banana

sleeve

tip

RCA

1/8"

Neutrik® Speakon®

Wiring Diagrams

When wiring your cables, be sure to do it right. If you are not comfortable in this department, use someone that is already pretty handy with a solder gun. Polarity and correct pin configurations are essential to know when venturing in the land of self-wired cables. Here's some help in that area.

Instrument/Patch Cable (mono)

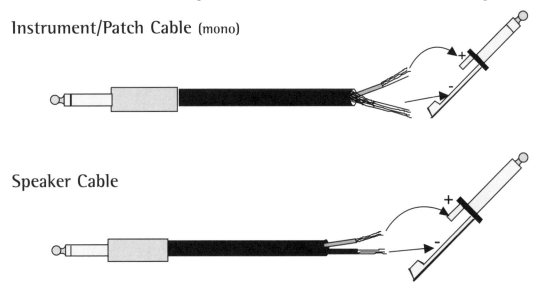

Speaker Cable

Microphone Cables

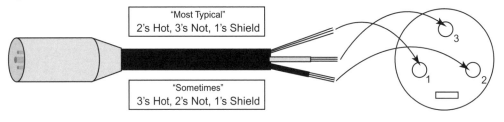

"Most Typical"
2's Hot, 3's Not, 1's Shield

"Sometimes"
3's Hot, 2's Not, 1's Shield

1/4" TRS   Tip = hot, Ring = neutral, Sleeve = ground

Banana   Ground side is labeled, other side is hot

RCA   Tip = hot, Sleeve = ground.

Part Two: Beyond the Basics "Putting What You Know to Work"

Now that you understand the basic components of a sound system, it's time for the good stuff: how to make your system work for you. We'll start by looking at the essentials of setting up your sound system. We'll then proceed to some invaluable tips that will help you avoid common pitfalls, troubleshoot any current problems you may be experiencing, and achieve the best possible sound in your church service.

chapter 4

Setting Up the Room

Feedback

Feedback is that ear-piercing, system-blowing, complaint-generating squeal and howl that appears in your sound system. Feedback is a guaranteed method of bringing attention to yourself—but who needs that kind of attention!

Feedback is the result of a loop of sound. Typically it involves sound from the speakers projecting into the pickup pattern of microphones. The sound from the speaker goes into the microphone and is re-amplified through the speakers, and that sound is again picked up by the microphone, and 'round and 'round it goes. So that's how feedback is created, now how do we make it go away?

First, we need to make sure that the speaker placement is as good as it can be (see "Speaker Placement" on page 18). Speakers set behind the microphones or facing into microphones will cause feedback.

Next, feedback is frequency-based, so if we can reduce the problem frequencies, we can control the feedback. This is where graphic equalizers come in real handy. With a graphic equalizer, you can identify the problem frequencies and reduce them until the feedback is gone. Each band (slider) of an equalizer controls a group of frequencies. Since we want to reduce feedback without affecting the quality of sound, a 31-band equalizer is preferred. A 31-band equalizer allows you to pull down narrower groups of frequencies than does a 15-band equalizer. This will allow you to pull down the problem frequency without pulling down too many non-problem frequencies. Although a 15-band equalizer will allow you to reduce problem frequencies, the innocent frequencies around it will also be reduced. This "guilt by association" treatment of frequencies can cause you to lose some of those sweet and warm frequencies just 'cause they were standing close to the bad guy. I'm not saying that 15-band equalizers aren't ever adequate, because for many applications they are. Even in those situations, I prefer 31 bands for potential or future needs, but this is not the most cost-effective approach.

Setting the EQ

Setting the equalizer is a crucial step to successful feedback control. This process is also called "ringing out the room." It is the process of reducing problem frequencies until the feedback

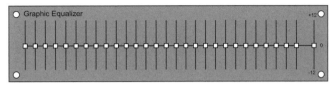

is gone. You will need to set the equalizers for mains and monitors. First set the main system EQ. Then use this same process for the monitors.

Step 1 –

Set up the microphones that are used during a service in the locations that they are used. This includes the lapel mics (clip them to a music stand to simulate the application) and any wireless mic that is used.

Step 2 –

On the mixer, set each channel's EQ settings to flat (the "0" position, no boosting or lowering of frequencies). Set all sliders of the graphic equalizer to the flat position.

Step 3 –

Choose a main microphone that must pick up from a distance such as a podium or lapel mic. Slowly and carefully bring its volume control up until you start to hear feedback. Keep your hand on the volume control so that the feedback does not get out of control. You want it to ring loud enough to hear the feedback but not blow anything, so be careful. To get the ringing started, have someone say "check" into the mic every 3-5 seconds.

Step 4 –

Keep one hand on the mixer and the other adjusting the equalizer. Find a problem frequency by keeping the feedback ringing, and first dropping, then replacing EQ frequency sliders one at a time until you find it. (Some EQs have locater lights above the frequency sliders to help you with this step.) Use your ears to narrow down the possibilities. If the feedback sounds high, then start trying the higher frequency sliders first. If it sounds low, then start there. You will find that more than one slider may reduce the feedback. Once you've found the sliders that get rid of the feedback, identify which one seems to most strongly reduce the feedback with the least amount of adjustment. Now turn down that slider till the feedback goes away.

Step 5 –

Repeat Step 4 until most of the problem frequencies are reduced.

Step 6 –

Start turning up other microphones one at a time, and repeat Step 4.

Remember that we want to reduce feedback with the least amount of adjustment. If you overadjust the EQ, you will be pulling down too many frequencies and therefore altering the whole sound of the system.

For sound reinforcement applications (that's you!), a graphic equalizer should *never* have any sliders set above the "0" mark. We are using the EQ to *remove* problems. Boosting any frequencies on the equalizer will create many problems. Do not try to enhance frequencies with this equalizer; chances are you will only enhance the likelihood of bad experiences.

Speaker Placement

Speaker placement may be the most important decision when designing a sound system. Your choice of placement determines the system's potential. Poor choices in this area can result in feedback, poor dispersion of sound, and many other "not-so-exciting" possibilities. The choice of placement is based on one premise: Project the sound to the ears of the congregation and not into the microphones. If you accomplish this, you will have a congregation that hears well and fewer feedback problems. There are other things that we want to also accomplish such as making it sound natural while keeping it aesthetically pleasing. Speakers act much like a flashlight. They project best in the direction they are pointed. When positioning speakers, it is helpful to use this flashlight parallel. Make sure that the congregation is "well lit."

1) Never place the speakers behind the microphones.

Placing speakers behind microphones will blow the sound directly into the pickup pattern of microphones and will therefore cause feedback.

Incorrect

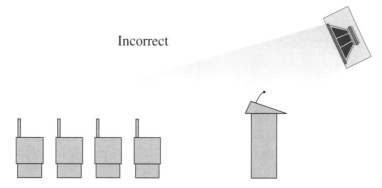

2) When possible, angle the speakers to project onto the congregation, not the back wall.

This means that the sound will be absorbed by, and projected directly to the people. This will help to keep the sound from bouncing around and causing that "echoy" jumbled sound.

Correct

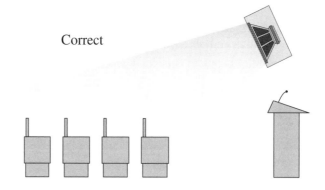

3) Place the speakers to simulate the sound coming from a single source.

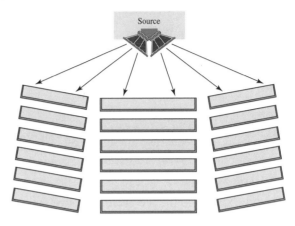

Human hearing is set up so that we sense an incoming sound's orientation by left, right, or center, but we are not as easily able to determine if the sound is coming from ground level or above. Because of this fact, it is most desirable to have a central cluster of speakers placed above the front platform area. Research says that this design gives the perception that the sound is coming directly from the source and therefore seems more natural.

Many times, this also means that you would be placing the speakers directly in front of a cross, the projector screen, or some other important item that cannot be obstructed. In this case, place the speakers so that they can best simulate the sound coming from a single source. (See the speaker placement options in this section.)

4) Set speaker height so that the high-frequency horn is above the congregation's heads when they are standing.

Unlike low frequencies, high frequencies are very directional. How many times have you heard the rumble of loud music coming from a car or building? You will notice that almost all of what you hear is bass frequencies. High frequencies don't travel through objects very well. As a rule, in order to effectively hear high frequencies, one must have a clear shot from the horn to the ears. Since high frequencies are largely responsible for clarity and intelligibility, it is really important to offer an unobstructed path of sound to the listener.

5) Use extra speakers only to fill in the holes.

The more sources of sound, the greater the possibility for jumbled sound. Use extra speakers only where necessary such as under balconies or dead spots. Sometimes these needs can only be determined after positioning the main system speakers.

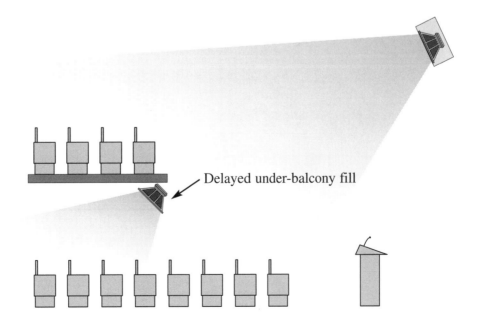

Delayed under-balcony fill

6) Place subwoofers carefully.

Although low-frequency speakers are less directional in their projection, the listener can tell their area of orientation. You want the sound to be even around the room and not blow away the person sitting near the subwoofer or draw their focus to it. Try to place the subwoofer(s) with, under, or as near as possible to the main speakers. This will help to make things sound more natural. Use one in the cluster or one on each side of the platform area. Again, do not place speakers behind or projecting into the microphones.

Speaker Placement Options

Central Cluster

This is considered the preferred option since it offers single-source configuration and good coverage. Make sure that the speaker cluster is above or beyond the front of the platform and aimed down at the congregation.

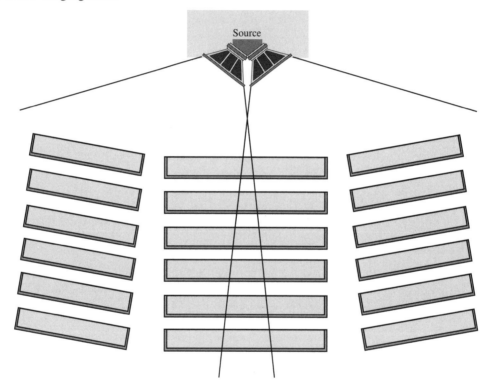

Simulated Single-Source

This option can be used to simulate the sound coming from a single source. Position the speakers so that sound appears to originate from a single point and projects outward.

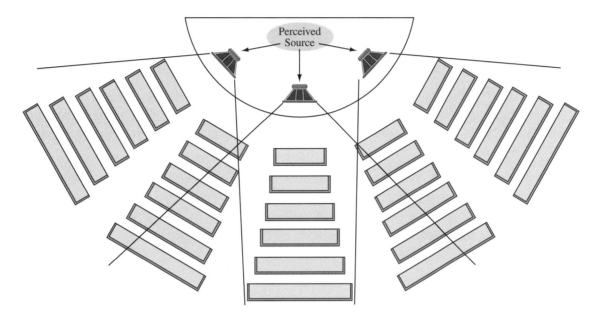

Split-Stack Configuration

When single-source applications can't be used, sometimes this is the best alternate choice. Aim speakers so that you get good coverage yet keep the platform area out of the coverage pattern.

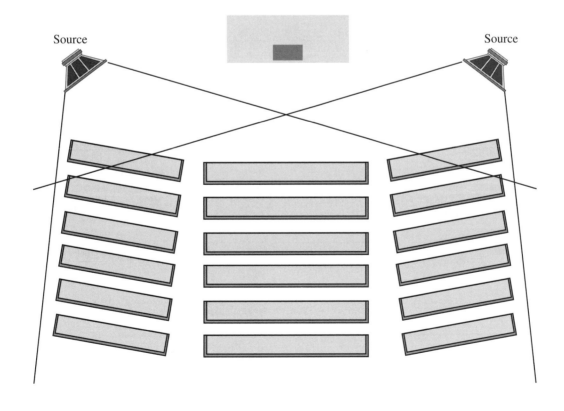

The Sound System Control Station

One question that I am frequently asked is, "Where should we put the control station?" The control station is the place that the mixer and most other components are kept, and this is where the sound person will be sitting during the service. My answer to this question is not always received with joy and jubilation. The best overall location is about 2/3 back and just off center in the sanctuary. In order for you to properly make adjustments to the sound, you will need to hear what the congregation hears. The best way to hear what the congregation hears is to be in the congregation.

If you are stuck in a sound booth or a closet, you have no idea what it sounds like in the sanctuary. Headphones, although a helpful tool, do not give true representation of the sound in the sanctuary. Window-like openings in a sound booth are an improvement (the bigger the better), but it still sounds significantly different than in the sanctuary.

In a church, it is not always possible or practical to have this ideal placement of the station. When you cannot put the control station in the ideal location, minimize your compromise. Build a wood cabinet for the equipment, put up pew height walls, move it to the back of the room, just avoid moving it out of the sanctuary. If you do end up in a booth, you will need to walk into the sanctuary during the services to ensure that the sound is what you think it is.

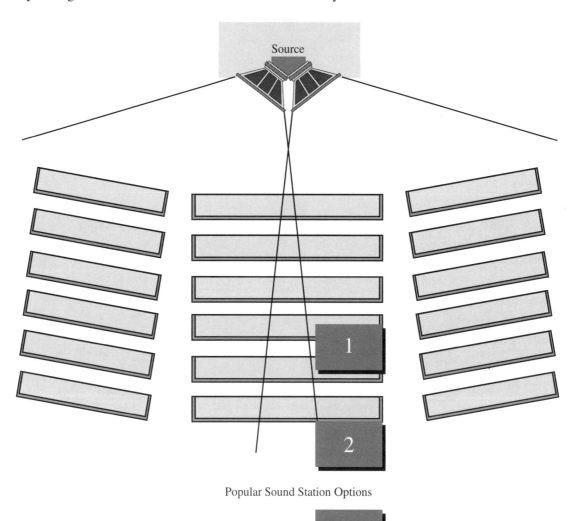

Popular Sound Station Options

chapter 5

Big Problem Solvers–Tips & Tricks

This is the section that will get you the most for your money. Now that you know what all this equipment is and what it does, we'll give you some do's and don'ts. This information will go a long way to making your system work efficiently and to its potential. Believe it or not, you are well on your way to being a well-informed sound person.

Microphone Use and Placement

When purchasing microphones, be sure to have specific duties in mind. Map out your needs; there are microphones for almost every application. Once you have the microphones, be sure to use them properly.

Position microphones so that speakers or monitors are not projecting into the face of the microphones. This will make all the difference in the world.

A microphone is not a sound-seeking unit. It picks up the sound that is coming into its pickup pattern. The closer the mic is to the sound source, the better it picks it up.

Vocal Microphones

The shy vocalist who stands a foot from their microphone will not be heard like the confident vocalist who gets right on their mic. That shy vocalist will also be the first to say that they cannot hear themselves through the system. Get your vocalists as close as you can to their microphone, and you will have the best tone, control, and the least amount of feedback. Also, when vocalists sing close and right into a microphone, the signal is more consistent. The sound will be less likely to be loud and quiet as they move around. Remind people that you are there for sound reinforcement and that they must provide you with a good strong sound.

Choir Microphones

Again be sure that there are no speakers projecting into these microphones. Since these mics pick up large areas, they are more susceptible to feedback. Don't put these mics into the monitor mix. Bring their respective volume controls up slowly during services, so that you can sense any feedback early enough to react. Place these mics close enough to pick up the whole group well. In my experience, this is usually a few feet in front of the first row and one to four feet above their heads. Most choirs require at least two mics. Use separate handheld mics for soloists.

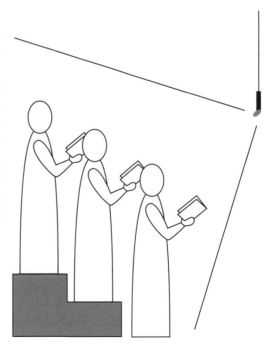

Lapel Microphones

Since a headset mic would probably be inappropriate, and people don't always want to hold a handheld microphone when they speak, lapel mics become a necessary tool. These microphones can be difficult to work with. Since the sound that you are attempting to amplify is projecting above and beyond the mic, it is difficult to capture that sound without also capturing some feedback. Proceed carefully with equalization since boosting frequencies can lead to feedback. Instead, use negative EQ adjustments to remove the undesirable characteristics of the sound (such as hollow or nasal tone). An example of this would be if a mic sounds "tinny," don't add bass, instead remove some highs or high-mids. The end result will be better sound without inviting feedback. Make sure that the mic is unobstructed by clothing and is aimed up toward the person's chin so that the sound will accommodate its pickup pattern.

Podium Microphones

Units designed specifically for this application are slender in profile and offer a generous pickup pattern. The result is a unobtrusive mic with good sound performance. This mic cannot, however, follow a person around and magically capture their voice. The person who wanders away from the podium mic is no longer speaking into it so...it ain't gonna pick up their voice real good, see! Avoid an omnidirectional mic unless it is specifically designed for this application (you may inherit a world of feedback when you try to turn it up).

Instrument Microphones

There are lots of different instruments that you may encounter. Every instrument has unique characteristics and requires different means of capturing its sound with microphones. For this reason, there are mics designed for most any application. In the changing environment of churches, it is good to have multi-application mics around. Since you are trying to zero in on the sound produced by a specific instrument, instrument microphones are usually unidirectional cardioid or supercardioid design. Just like a vocal mic, proximity is important. Get the mic nice and close, and point it directly at the sweet-sounding spot of the instrument.

Wireless Systems

Wired microphones and instruments have a cable directly attached for the sound to travel through. That's a pretty secure environment to travel through without much interference. Wireless systems for instruments and microphones rely on the sound traveling from a transmitting unit, through the air, and to a receiver without a scratch. This is the electronic equivalent of being shot out of a cannon, through the woods, and into a hammock at the other end. Chances are you may end up bouncing off a tree someday. When choosing a wireless system, especially if it is to be used for delivering the message, don't shop out of the budget bin. This is not the place to trim the expenses. There is plenty of potential interference out there that you will be battling; make sure that you are properly armed. Look for brands with track records and good reputation.

Diversity systems (systems using dual antennae and receivers) switch between two receivers, and you're less likely to encounter interference. Don't get me wrong; there have been plenty of situations where a single antenna VHF wireless is enough for the job, but if budget allows, go diversity.

There are two frequency ranges that wireless systems broadcast in, UHF and VHF. Much to the surprise of many, one is not discernibly better than the other when it comes to sound quality. This is simply which electronic highway the sound travels through to get to the other end, each having their own strengths and weaknesses. UHF systems are known for fewer incidence of interference since there is not nearly as much activity in that frequency range. UHF systems, however, are not very good at traveling through walls and objects, so be sure that the transmitters and receivers are line of sight. VHF systems, on the other hand, are pretty forgiving when it comes to going around corners and through walls. Unfortunately, there is more activity in VHF frequencies so there is usually more potential for outside interference.

In order for a wireless system to work at its best, make sure you take all the precautions you can. If you follow these rules you should get the most out of your system.

1) Keep a fresh battery in your transmitter at all times. Weak batteries don't provide enough power to transmit a strong signal.

2) Use the same brand alkaline battery consistently. The contact tabs in a battery compartment bend to fit the battery snugly. Since the size of different models of batteries all vary slightly, the battery may not have a tight fit if you switch brands and models.

3) Avoid rechargeable batteries.

4) Keep the receiver away from things that emit RF (radio frequencies) or you will be sure to have some form of interference. These are things such as CD players, digital processors (or anything else digital for that matter), amplifiers, and so on. Just to be safe, it is a good idea to keep your receivers at least four feet away from that type of equipment.

To mic a...	Use a...	Put it...	Hint/comment	Monitor tip
Vocal soloist	Handheld cardioid mic	Touching lips or as close to their mouth as they feel comfortable.	They must be close for good quality and consistency.	Vocalist should face the monitor and keep mic from facing monitor.
Roaming speaker	Handheld wireless mic	Touching lips or as close to their mouth as they feel comfortable.	Handheld mics are typically better at feedback rejection than lapel mics.	Safe to put through monitors same as for soloist.
Roaming speaker who does not want to carry a handheld	Wireless lapel unidirectional or omnidirectional	On tie or lapel, up high about eight to ten inches from the mouth.	Be careful: If they try to walk beyond the main speakers, the mic may feed back. Unidirectional mics are less likely to cause feedback.	Do not run lapel mics through monitors. Monitor use may induce feedback.
Choir or large vocal group	Low-profile unidirectional cardioid or hypercardioid condenser hanging mic.	One to four feet above and a few feet in front of the front choir row. Aim at the center of the area you are trying to pick up.	Use one mic for every 10 to 20 people. Most applications would benefit from at least two mics.	Do not run choir mics through monitors. Monitor use may induce feedback. Put musical accompaniment and soloists through the choir's monitors for their reference.
Grand piano Option #1	Unidirectional cardioid mic.	About a foot above the middle strings and 6 to 10 inches from the hammer area pointing down with lid full-stick.	Every piano sounds different; you may need to move the microphone around to find the sweet spot.	Place monitor so that it is facing the player but not the piano microphone.
Grand piano Option #2	Pair of flat surface mount mics.	Attached to the closed lid and positioned over strings to get the most even sound possible.	Every piano sounds different; you may need to move the microphone around to find the sweet spot.	Place monitor so that it is facing the player but not the piano microphone.
Upright piano with one mic	Unidirectional cardioid mic	Just above the lid over the high strings or 6 to 12 inches from the center of the back of the piano (sound board).	Every piano sounds different; you may need to move the microphone around to find the sweet spot.	Place monitor so that it is facing the player but not the piano microphone.
Upright piano with two mics.	Pair of unidirectional cardioid mics.	Just above the open piano lid, spread for even coverage.	Every piano sounds different; you may need to move the microphone around to find the sweet spot.	Place monitor so that it is facing the player but not the piano microphone.

To mic a...	Use a...	Put it...	Hint/comment	Monitor tip
Acoustic guitar	Unidirectional cardioid mic.	A few inches from the soundhole or use a clip-on mic inside or outside the soundhole.	Playing styles vary, so mic to accomodate individual style and sound.	Bleed through the monitors, but be careful: Feedback is not hard to find in this application.
Brass	Unidirectional cardioid mic.	Use a clip-on mic on the bell, or a mic a few inches from the bell.	You may not need to turn them up much since they are so naturally loud.	Place monitor facing player. You may bleed the brass mics in if necessary.
Flute	Unidirectional cardioid mic.	A few inches away between the mouth and the fingers.	This sound will cut through the mix nicely but watch out for shrill tones.	You should not need much flute in the monitors. Bring them in only if necessary.
Instrument amplifiers	Unidirectional cardioid mic.	Close to speaker just off center.	Move the mic around a bit to find the sweet spot. The closer to the center of the speaker, the brighter the sound.	Players should use their amplifiers to hear themselvesr. You can bleen them through the monitors if others need to hear them.
Electronic organ with Leslie or tone cabinet	Unidirectional cardioid mic.	One or two mics on the tweeter and one on the woofer.	So many designs, no way to specifically address all types.	Organist usually will hear themselves well without monitors.
Snare and tom drums	Unidirectional cardioid mic.	Over edge of top heads facing down.	Two toms can share a mic; place the mic between them.	Drums are usually loud enough acoustically. Drummers usually need the monitors to help them hear everyone else.
Kick drum	Unidirectional cardioid, large diaphragm if possible.	In center of drum facing the beater.	Create tighter sounds by placing a pillow in the drum touching both heads.	Drums are usually loud enough acoustically. Drummers usually need the monitors to help them hear everyone else.
Cymbals	Unidirectional cardioid, condenser preferred.	Two overhead to pick up all cymbals, and in larger settings, one each on high-hat and ride.	These mics won't need to be turned up very loud to be effective. Use them to round out the sound.	Don't put these mics in the monitor mix.

The Mixer

1) Gain

Set each channel's gain so that you get good strong signal without peaking or distortion. Too weak of a signal will introduce unwanted noise and hiss. Too strong of a signal will cause clipping and distortion. Keep it between the lines. Use your solo buttons to check the level on the meter. When set properly, your meters should read close to 0 dB for the average signal strength.

2) Channel EQ

If you are setting any of your EQ knobs past 2 o'clock, be careful. Chances are good that you are overdoing it, and you may add to problems such as feedback or clipping. Use negative EQ whenever possible to eliminate the undesirable attributes of the sound. As a rule, don't boost midrange frequencies; although they give the illusion of increased sound, it is usually not a good sound.

3) Aux Sends

Use pre-fader sends for monitors and post-fader sends for effects. When needing more than one monitor mix, use a separate aux send for each group of monitors. Use post-fader sends also for needs like a recording output or an additional feed that can be affected by fader movement.

Never use an aux send for things that need to alter the entire signal, such as equalizers or compressors. These types of signal processors should be patched into the **inserts** or from the main outputs.

4) Subgroups and Other Assignments

Subgroups, also called **buses**, are a great tool that can help make running the system a bit easier. It is a good idea to assign channels to groups that pertain to certain segments of your service. Every church does things a little differently, so cater your groups for the particular needs of your church. For instance, assign the worship team to two subgroups, one for vocals and one for instruments. When the worship team is done with their portion of the service, you will be able to turn them down until they are needed again. Assign the speaker's lapel mics and other mics used for speech to a subgroup so that you can have them off until needed. Assuming you have a four-bus mixer, this will leave you with one for playback devices or any other leftovers.

Another neat trick is to assign things that utilize the benefits of the subwoofer to a subgroup, and hook the subwoofer system to its output. This keeps unwanted sources that don't need the subwoofer system, like the pastors lapel mic, from going through it. It also becomes a volume control for the subwoofer at your fingertips.

If you have multiple people running the sound system at various times, make sure that everyone works the system the same way. Many times a specific sound person will have assigned channels to groups, and left it that way. The next sound person that arrives and is not used to using subgroups will not be able to make the system work. I recommend that you either use them consistently or bypass them altogether to avoid the confusion.

5) Solo/Mute

When you press the solo button, it singles that channel out in your headphones. This comes in really handy when you are trying to find problems in the middle of the service. In this way, you can listen to specific sources one at a time without affecting what the congregation hears.

The solo button has another handy function in many mixers. On some models, when you solo a channel it shows the signal of that channel on the master meters. This allows you to set the gains for each channel, one at a time of course, by using the meters to precisely see your signal strength.

The mute button shuts off the channel. Use it to turn off channels when not in use. This comes in handy because it also shuts the mic off through the monitor and effect sends. When you turn down a subgroup to turn off mics, their respective monitor sends are still hot. The most often made mistake in this area is forgetting to turn the mute off and wondering why you get no sound.

6) Faders

If your gain structure is set properly, all of the channel's faders should be around three quarters of the way up. This gives you a little room to turn up and down if you need to, and also gives you the proper amount of signal coming through the system. Of course, when mixing the sound, all faders will not always be at the exact same position. You can move them to blend the sound to sweeten the mix.

7) Master Volume

Again, if your gain structure is set properly, all of the channel's faders should be around three quarters of the way up, and this goes for your master faders also. If you don't have good gain structure on the mixer, your meters won't register well, and all of your outputs may be weak.

Graphic Equalizers

Never set any sliders above the zero setting that is in the middle. Use these units to remove problems, not to sweeten the sound.

Amplifiers

There are a couple of schools of thought when it comes to this. Some say leave your power amplifiers on full volume at all times, while others say to back them down.

Leaving the amplifiers at full power gives you full control from the mixer to reach the amplifiers maximum potential. However, this may also leave your system with a noticeable hiss when it is idle.

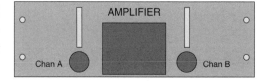

The other approach is to set the amplifiers so that they are at a comfortable volume when your mixer's faders, both channel and master, are all at the 0 dB or unity gain setting. You can experiment with this and choose what is best.

Also, be sure that your amplifier has adequate ventilation to cool itself. If the amps get hot they may shut down or burn out.

Mono, Stereo, and Bridged

As discussed before, there are two types of amplifiers: **mono** and **stereo**.

Mono amplifiers are simply units containing one amplifier. This means that they have only one amplifier channel. Although this is a less popular style of stand-alone amplifier, they are commonly used in powered mixers or to power smaller systems. Since they are mono, be sure not to parallel too many speakers off of the amplifier. Use the suggestions in the next section for safe use.

Stereo amplifiers are units with two amplifiers sometimes labeled channel A and channel B. Each channel has its own inputs, outputs, and volume control.

A **mono bridged** option is also available on some amplifiers. This allows you to combine the two channels of a stereo amplifier to make it one big mono amplifier with the flip of a switch. Be sure to read your manual before you bridge an amplifier. Most amplifiers have minimum ohm requirements. Very few amplifiers will run lower than a 4-ohm load comfortably in bridge mode. This means that you can either run (in a parallel chain) one 4-ohm cabinet, or no more than two 8-ohm cabinets off of the amplifier. Also, many models require you to connect the speaker wires to the two positive (red) speaker terminals using a banana connector or bare wires.

You may also see the term **dual mono** or **parallel**. This simply means that if you plug something into one channel (usually channel A) it will also send that signal over to the other channel. This way you can use both sides of the amplifier with a single input. Since a single input (mono) is being amplified out of both channels, they call it dual mono.

One other type of system you may encounter is a **25-** or **70-volt system**. You can use this system when a whole bunch of little low-volume speakers are need. They require the use of a transformer on each speaker and an amplifier that will accommodate the specs of the transformers (25-volt or 70-volt usually). Each transformer can be wired at different wattages, such as 5 or 10 watts. When you add up the wattages of all the speakers that you have wired, this will tell you the size of the amp needed. For example, if you have ten speakers wired at ten watts, you need at least a 100-watt amplifier (10 speakers X 10 watts = 100-watt amp needed).

Speakers

Speaker Chains and Impedance

On the back of many speaker cabinets are more than one input, called **parallel** inputs. (Don't confuse this with wiring speakers in **series**.) These inputs allow you to chain together more than one speaker. This is not, however, an infinite freedom. If you chain too many speakers together, it overworks the amplifier and will cause it to fail. In order to safely run this part of your system, you will need to find out a couple specs. You will need one spec from your speakers and one from your amp, both related to ohms.

An **ohm** is the unit of measurement used to quantify the amount of opposition to a current's flow through a circuit. This rating is the speakers **impedance**. Amplifiers deliver different wattages to the speakers depending on their impedance. Most speaker cabinets are 8-ohms although some cabinets are 4- or 16-ohms. They are usually labeled on the back of the cabinet near the input jacks. Near the speaker outputs on the amplifier, there should be a "minimum ohm rating" listed for each channel. It will read something like "4-ohms minimum load." Find out this spec, and then you'll be able to determine how many speakers you can run off each amplifier channel.

There are formulas to follow when figuring out how many speakers you can chain together. Rather than delve into the formula approach, follow these rules and run safe.

If your amp says 2-ohm min. load per channel:

1) Don't chain more than four 8-ohm speakers together on one channel.

2) Don't connect more than two 4-ohm speakers to a channel.

If your amp says 4-ohm min. load per channel:

1) Don't chain more than two 8-ohm speakers together on one channel.

2) Don't connect more than one 4-ohm speaker to a channel.

Speaker Choices

Just like every other component in your system, there are plenty of makes and models to choose from when it comes to speakers. You will need to consider your present as well as your potential needs. Make sure that, as your services grow and change, you have speakers that are able to accommodate that growth. The main things to look at when buying speakers is the size of the woofer and the design of the horn. The look, of course, is a nice bonus.

The larger the woofer, the greater the bass frequency reproduction. Within sizes are different qualities and power handling, so research manufacturer and models to be sure that they can do the job. If you are using the speaker just for voice amplification, you should not need a greater than 12" woofer. If you are using the system for music and speech, then you probably need a 12" or 15" speaker in the system. If you want to reproduce sound that has powerful low frequencies, you will want speaker cabinets with at least a 15" woofer. This will help reproduce those frequencies that instruments create like the pedal tones of a pipe organ sound, or a kick drum. If you will need this range of frequencies at significant volumes, you could add a subwoofer. This will allow your congregation to not only hear the sound but also feel it.

The tweeter is the component that provides the high-frequencies of the sound system. These frequencies determine the clarity of music and intelligibility of the spoken word. There are a couple of choices of which to be aware.

A **piezoelectric** tweeter is typically inexpensive and can do the job in many situations. They are not known for long throws of the sound or extended frequency reproduction but are a great source for economical high frequency reproduction.

If you have a large sanctuary, cabinets with a horn driver are probably best. These come in 1" and 2" configurations. They are very good with extended frequency handling and with sound projection. They are known for being a clearer sounding, longer-throwing design, but of course there is a cost for this advantage.

Depending on the width and layout of your sanctuary, you will need varying numbers of cabinets in your cluster (or other design) in order to get complete coverage.

Monitors

Don't run too many monitors off of one channel of an amplifier. This will keep your amp from being overworked. Use the advice from the Speaker Chain and Impedance section of this book on p. 30.

Set monitors so that the people using them can see the base of the horn on the monitor. If they can see it, they can hear it. If they can't, they will not hear the high frequencies very well. Even though the monitor may be loud, if they can't hear the high frequencies, the perception is that they cannot hear themselves. You will turn them up until everyone complains that they are too loud, and they will still not hear themselves. This is because all the definition of the sound comes from those higher frequencies. If the performers cannot hear properly, they will have a hard time with pitch, timing, and feel for the music.

Try to get your monitor mix to the point that the musicians and vocalists can concentrate on their own performance and not that of the system.

Recording and Playback Devices

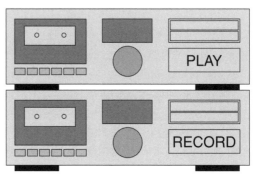

You will be wise to get at least two units for these applications. You have two separate jobs that you are trying to do: Record the service and play music. If you try to do both with one deck, chances are really good that you will end up with a feedback loop and cause a loud squealing howl in the middle of the service. You may even blow components of your system, and the repair bill will far exceed the cost of buying a second unit. Your recording deck will be connected to one of a couple of places on your mixer. Many mixers have tape outputs; these certainly would be the first choice. You can also hook your recording deck to a master out or an aux out.

In situations where you want to record a mix that is different than your main mix, use an aux send. With an aux send, you can adjust the level of each channel separately to create your recording mix.

Sometimes it makes for a more realistic sound on the recording if you put a couple of mics over the congregation and add them sparingly to your recording mix. This way you will hear everything in the room as if you were there and not just the sound of the mics on the platform. Do not use this technique if you don't have a separate recording mix. The congregation mics will be in a direct line of the speakers, and if they are brought up in the main mix, they will feed back.

Other Suggestions

1. Provide good air circulation for your equipment so that it can stay cool.
2. Organize all cables, and keep power cables separate if possible.
3. Have your sound company do a semiannual service call to keep it running smoothly.
4. Put security covers on system EQs and crossovers to protect their settings.
5. Turn on power amps lost during power up and off first at power down.
6. Check wireless power switches after every service to save batteries.
7. When recording, set recording levels as high as you can without distortion. Also use a chrome bias tape as your master.
8. Have an electrician provide separate circuits with isolated grounds and neutrals for the sound system. This will minimize any chance for hums and electrical noises.

chapter 6

Where and How to Buy Your Equipment

This is a really important step in the process. Who you buy from will have a lasting effect on how your sound system performs.

You must seek out a qualified business that deals with churches regularly—one that understands not only sound but churches and their various worship styles and needs. These are the people who will be making recommendations, giving advice, and servicing your equipment. You now know the basics of what you need; they will be showing you makes and models that are available.

Don't shop based on price alone. You may find that mail order or internet prices are cheaper, but that's because they sell products only. When the mic doesn't sound right, or there's a buzz that won't go away, or the system just plain won't work, a mail order catalog won't be of much help. Will they be able to offer loaners to replace items in need of service, or offer on-site recommendations and training? Your local or regional business will be advising and servicing you, and that is worth more than most realize. Let the local business know that you need them to be competitive, but want the services that they can offer. You may pay a little more, but you'll end up with a better running system and a better understanding of it. For a church, these things do matter.

Request references, and follow them up. This will definitely help you to weed out the bad choices and maybe even get you some referrals.

Part Three:
A Worship Team Manual
for Better Sound

Now that you are familiar with the sound system basics and are on the road to better sound, remember that you are reinforcing the "sound." The next step is to make sure that the sound that you are reinforcing is as good as it can be. A bad sound through a sound system is just a louder bad sound. You will need to work hand in hand with the worship team and clergy in order to effectively accomplish a good sound consistently.

The following pages are a handout that you should give to each member of the worship team as well as anyone else involved in the service. This handout will help to show what each member can do to contribute to the smooth function of the sound and the service.

Worship Service
Team Manual for Better Sound

Typically the function of a Worship Service Team is to lead the congregation in musical worship and to prepare their hearts and minds for the message to follow. As simple as this important job seems, if there are audio problems, the worship team will not be able to perform comfortably. The goal of the sound crew is to ensure you have the best sound possible with the equipment provided. This will require a group effort, by all members of the team.

The following tips are a list of requests and suggestions for each member of the team. If you subscribe to these suggestions, the result will be better sound and a better service. It will also help to make everyone more comfortable in their respective assignments.

Vocalists

Please stay close and consistent to your microphones. This will help the sound person to keep your volume and tone consistent and help you to hear yourself through the monitors. Don't be shy. The mic cannot chase your voice around; you have to make the sound go into your mic. Try to keep your mouth close to the mic at all times, and back off only when you sing exceptionally louder than normal. If you "work the mic" as some more seasoned vocalists do, only do so in order to deliver a consistent volume to the system.

Stand so that the monitors are facing directly at you. If you seem too loud or soft through the monitors, first make sure that you are close and consistent with the mic. If you are still having trouble, ask a sound person to make adjustments.

If you are sharing stage monitors, arrange yourselves so that the speaker is directly facing all vocalists. For best results, try not to exceed two people per monitor (choirs exempt).

Keyboardists

If you have an amplifier, try placing it so that it is aimed right at your face. Raise it or tip it back if necessary. Set your volume so that you can hear yourself clearly but are not overbearing to the rest of the members. Use a direct box to interface with the sound system.

Guitarists

If you have an amplifier, placing it in front of you or just off to the side may help to keep stage volumes low while still hearing yourself well. Tip back the amp or raise it so that it is aimed right at your face. Set your volume so that you can hear yourself clearly but are not overbearing to the rest of the members. Guitar amps tend to be extremely directional, so be aware of where your amp is pointing.

To get the guitar into the system, use the following: For electric guitar amps, use a microphone facing the speaker just off the center. For acoustic guitars with electronics, use a direct box. Otherwise, use a mic near the soundhole.

Bass Players

If you have an amplifier for monitoring but are also amplified through the sound system, try placing your amp in front of you or just of to the side and tipped back so that it is aimed right at your face. This will help to control stage volumes while still allowing you to hear yourself. Set your volume so that you can hear yourself clearly but are not overbearing to the rest of the members.

Bass frequencies travel omnidirectionally and can quickly become too loud for the congregation, and those around you, so be aware of your stage volume. If you're using only your amp with no additional reinforcement from the sound system, set your amp behind you facing the congregation, but aimed so that you get good monitoring from the amp. Because of the nature of bass frequencies and the size of their wavelenth, your amp may not seem loud to you, but it still may be too loud for those farther away. Sometimes tipping the amp back or elevating it so that it is aimed at your ears can resolve the problem.

Use a direct box to interface with the sound system.

Drummers

Drums are designed to be hit—after all, they are drums! And many times they sound best when hit hard! To get in "the pocket" and feel the music, drummers prefer to hit at their comfort level. With that said and understood, the fact is that the comfort level of the congregation and those around you is paramount. The drums do play a vital support role in a worship team, but it is unlike that of bands outside a church setting. Drums and percussion instruments are the adhesive of the music that pulls everything together.

Remember to play with great respect for those around you. It will be a challenge to play such a dynamic instrument with finesse, but it will make all the difference in the world. You will find that you will be a significant contributor to mixing problems if your volume is too high. Drums are loud by the nature of their design. You may need to modify your technique slightly and/or use brushes or other tone control devices to decrease the volume. Many times the acoustic volume of the drums makes it difficult for others to hear their own performance, and then stage volumes keep creeping up until they are unmanageable. Play so that you blend with the stage volumes of the other instruments; this will benefit everyone. Use an electronic set for the best of both worlds—you will be able to hit with a comfortable force while having complete control of volume.

Aim your monitor directly at your ear. Elevate your monitor if needed.

Horn Players

Chances are very good that you won't need much in the way of amplification. Horns usually project well on their own. Remember that the sound comes out of the bell of your instruments in a directional way. Make sure that you are pointing the bell in a direction that will not blow anyone away.

Choirs

Ignore the sound system; don't count on it to fix volume or blending problems of the choir. Blend yourselves. Most choirs have a few vocalists who are significantly louder than the rest. Don't be shy, but don't overpower (unless requested by your choir director). The sound system will reinforce the sound that the group as a whole gives. The choir director will have the best sense of your blend, so be open to his or her suggestions.

Soloists who use a solo mic should follow the same suggestions as the vocalists.

Sound People

Listen carefully to the needs of the rest of the worship team. You are there to support them and then give the congregation the best mix that you can.

Everyone

Develop hand signals that will help you communicate with your sound person in the middle of the service without the congregation being distracted.

Keep stage volumes low so that the sound person has adequate control. Set your volumes just loud enough for you to be comfortable, not to project the sound to anyone else. Let the sound system amplify those sounds for you. Avoid volume wars.

Communicate. If you have a problem with anything, find a tactful way to discuss it. Be receptive to comments and criticism. The goal is to better the unit, not to insult. Communication is the best way to better the group and yourself as musicians and/or vocalists.

Work individually for the good of the whole.

glossary

Terms of Audio Endearment

The following section will give brief descriptions of terms and items that you will be likely to encounter. This will help you to not only better understand sound systems, but better express yourself when discussing the subject. The definitions given are far from a technical manual script, but are written to be helpful for your work with the sound system.

amplifier – By broad definition, a device that increases the power of a signal. In your sound system, it is the unit to which the speakers are directly hooked. It boosts the signal put into it and pumps that signal through your speakers. Its power is measured in watts.

attenuator – A knob or fader that facilitates changes to level or tone.

aux send – An option on mixers that allows you to send out a separate ("auxiliary") mix to things such as stage monitors, recording devices, and effect units. This is accomplished by adjusting the aux send knob on each individual channel to get the desired mix.

balanced line – Cables that utilize two conductors and a shield. This enables the line to run farther without interference or added noise.

biamp – A two-way sound system that splits the audio signal by frequency and utilizes separate amplifiers for lows and highs.

bridged mono – A stereo amplifier set to combine both amps into a single larger amp. In this way, the two amps that were separate are now bridged as one.

bus – Also called a group or subgroup, a bus allows you to group inputs and make adjustments to them as a group. For instance, you could set up all the vocal microphones in one group and all the instruments are another. In this way, you could control the volume of multiple inputs with one knob or slider (these sliders are commonly referred to as faders).

cardioid microphone – Microphone whose heart-shaped pickup pattern is sensitive to sound coming from the front and sides.

CD player – Compact disc player. Because of their digital sound quality and the available library of music, theses units are a popular choice for music playback.

clipping – The state at which an overdriven signal results in distortion. Some mixing consoles have clip indicators on channels to warn you when this occurs.

cluster – See "speaker cluster."

compression driver – A mid- and/or high-frequency electromagnetic speaker that uses a large magnet structure in its design.

compressor – A unit used to control signal levels by not allowing them to exceed a set point. This keeps levels from being too soft and then too loud. Compressors are good for protecting sound systems from sudden peaks in levels like yelling or an instrumentalist's overzealous performance.

condenser microphone – A microphone design that requires a power source ("phantom power") to function. This power can come from a battery or from a phantom power device.

crossover – A unit that splits up an audio signal by frequency in order to distribute it to the proper speaker or output transducer.

dB, decibel – The unit of measure used to define the power of acoustic or electronic signals. One-tenth of a Bel, named after Alexander Graham Bell.

DSP, digital signal processor – An electronic device that digitally alters an audio signal. Examples are reverb units and effect processors.

dynamic microphone – A popular and durable microphone design that transfers acoustic energy into an electronic signal. Works like a mini-speaker in reverse.

equalizer, EQ – Adjusts the tone of a signal. Simple designs offer a bass and treble control while others allow more detailed control. Equalizers appear on mixers, channels, or as stand-alone "outboard" processors. Used to "sweeten" the sound or to reduce the resonant frequencies that cause feedback by dipping the level of problem frequencies.

feedback – Occurs when a signal travels in a loop. For instance, when sound that is going into a microphone comes out of a speaker, and that sound goes back into the microphone, back out the speaker, looping and looping. The result is squealing and howling and other crowd-clearing noises. Unless you are a rock guitarist, this is not a good thing.

frequency – A frequency is a wave form whose repeating cycle creates a tone. Measured by how many times its cycle repeats per second. Sometimes referred to in groups such as low frequencies (bass) and high frequencies (treble).

gain – A control that usually increases or decreases the level of a signal. The term is also used to refer to a signal's strength, expressed in dB. Too much gain results in distortion, and not enough results in too much noise.

gain structure – A term used to describe the interaction of the gain settings throughout a system.

gate – These devices are electronic gateways through which the sound passes or is stopped depending on its strength. A gate is used to shut off unwanted noise.

graphic equalizer – An EQ with multiple controls, called "bands," that control set frequencies. Each band can boost or lower its designated frequency.

ground loop – Resulting in a hum or added noise, a ground loop occurs when several grounds exist between units.

headroom – The useable area between normal operating levels and the point that you experience overload. The more headroom the better.

hertz, Hz – The measurement of frequency, or how many times a cycle repeats per second. (Also, what occurs when you drop a speaker on your foot!) One hertz is one cycle per second while 1 kilohertz, kHz is 1,000 cycles per second. Human hearing range is considered to be from 20 Hz to 20 kHz. (Did you know that adult women can usually hear higher frequencies than men the same age? That answers a lot, huh!)

hypercardioid, supercardioid microphone – A highly directional microphone that picks up best from the direct front. It is a variation of the cardioid mic. This design boasts excellent rejection of sounds from the sides, but does pick up some sound from directly in the back.

impedance – The opposition in an electrical circuit to the flow of a current or circuit. This opposition is expressed in ohms. You will find speakers that are 4-, 8-, and 16-ohms. You will find inputs and outputs of devices labeled low or high impedance.

insert – A jack found on a mixer that is used as a send and return in one jack. Usually found on channels, it allows you to send the signal from that channel through a signal processor (EQ, compressor, etc.). Unlike aux sends, the insert puts the processor directly into the signal path.

insert cable – A cable used for inserts with a 1/4" TRS connector at one end (to plug into the insert jack) and two mono 1/4" connectors at the other end (one input and one output connected to a signal processor).

jack – A female connector designed to receive a male connector (plug). Example: You "plug" in your headphones into the headphone "jack." (also, Jill's accessory.)

limiter – A unit designed to limit the level that a signal can reach. Compared to an electrical ceiling that the signal cannot jump past. This helps control volume surges and to keep spikes in the signal from damaging equipment.

line level – An input or output level for a device that is typically -10 dB or +4dB and uses 1/4", 1/8" or RCA connectors. Examples of equipment that operate at line level are keyboards, tape decks, and CD players.

mono – Abbreviation for monaural. Refers to the use of one master channel as opposed to stereo, which uses two.

mute – A button on a channel of a mixer that allows you to turn that channel off.

noise gate – Electronic gateway through which sound passes or is stopped depending on its strength. The threshold at which the gate opens and closes is user-controllable.

ohm – The unit of measure used to describe impedance, the opposition in an electrical circuit to the flow of a current.

omnidirectional microphone – A microphone that picks up sound from all directions.

pan – A knob on a channel that assigns its output to a left or right master channel. On a mixer that has subgroups or buses, this knob aids in those assignments. (Also, something that you cook bacon in.)

patch cable – A shielded cable used to connect audio equipment. Don't use (unshielded) speaker cables for (shielded) patch cables; the shield is important to proper function.

phantom power – The power (usually 9 to 52 volts DC) that condenser microphones require in order to operate. Some microphones use a battery for that power while many mixers have this option built in. Stand-alone phantom power sources are also available.

phone connector – A 1/4" connector seen most often in professional audio applications. They are used for guitars, keyboards, speakers, and other electronic equipment.

phono or RCA connector – A two-conductor connector most commonly used for home audio equipment. You will find them on cassette decks and CD players.

pink noise – A test signal that is often used when setting the equalizers in a system. It sounds much like a rushing waterfall, and when properly used with a spectrum analyzer, it helps to identify problem frequencies.

plug – A male connector designed to interface with a female jack. (Also, helps to keep the water in the tub.)

polar pattern – The graphic depiction of the pickup pattern of a microphone or dispersion of a speaker.

polarity – Refers to a signal's direction of flow from positive to negative. The proper wiring of speakers, mics, and circuits relies greatly on determination of polarity.

potentiometer – A knob, slider, or fader that can be used to make adjustments such as volume and tone.

pre- and post-fader send – Sends on a mixer that allow you to route signal from a channel to additional places like monitor systems and effect units. The pre and post designations determine if the signal being sent is affected by fader movements. Typically pre-fader sends, which are not affected by fader adjustments, are used for monitor sends. Post-fader sends, which are affected by fader movement, are usually used for effect sends and other auxiliary uses.

rack mount – An industry standard size for equipment that is to be housed in a "rack." One "rack space" is approx 1¾" (H) x 19" (W).

resonance – This occurs when a frequency is emphasized by certain variables. A room may have certain resonant frequencies due to its dimensions and layout. It is at these resonant frequencies that your sound system is likely to feed back.

reverberation – When you clap your hands in a gymnasium, you will hear the sound continue for a period of time. What you are hearing is sound bouncing off the walls, floor, and ceiling and reflecting back to you. This is reverberation. Variables that determine the characteristics of reverberation are size of room, reflective surfaces and sound-absorbing materials (carpet, curtains, furniture). Reverb can be a desirable effect for vocals and instruments and can be simulated with the use of effect processors. Too much reverb can cause muddy sound and feedback. Related terms: DSP

ribbon microphone – A rarely seen type of dynamic microphone that uses a thin ribbon-like element. These are delicate microphones but have excellent studio-friendly characteristics.

shelving – A type of EQ where a knob controls a set group of frequencies like bass or treble. (Also, something to keep books and knickknacks on.)

shield – An uncoated wire that surrounds the coated wires in a shielded cable. It "shields" the audio signal passing through from outside interference.

signal processor – A term used to describe any device that manipulates the audio signal in some way. Examples are equalizers, compressors, limiters, effect processors, etc.

signal-to-noise ratio – Represents the difference between a signal's level and the level of the inherent noise in a circuit (hiss and hum-type stuff). The object of the game is to have a very low level of noise as compared to the signal. Too much noise in your system means that you will have annoying hiss and hum in your sound system.

solo – This is a feature on some mixers that allows you to select and listen to channels (and sometimes groups or sends) through your headphones or other monitoring devices. It is really helpful when trying to troubleshoot; for instance, when you need to find out who's singing flat so that you can turn them down.

speaker cluster – One or more speaker cabinets. Typically flown (hung with chain or rigging cable) centered above the front of the platform area and aimed down at the congregation.

stereo – Refers to the use of two master audio channels, typically left and right.

TRS – The abbreviation for "**Tip, Ring**, and **Sleeve**." These connectors are typically 1/4" in a pro-audio environment and are used to connect headphones or for channel inserts (incorporates a send and return in one jack), or as a balanced cable.

transducer – Something that transforms energy from one form to another. For example, a microphone changes acoustic energy into electrical energy, and a speaker does the opposite.

tweeter – A speaker designed for reproducing high (treble) frequencies.

watt – The unit of measure for electrical power dissipation. In a sound system, a power amplifier's strength is defined in watts.

waveform – A graphic depiction of a signal's changes in amplitude over time. A picture of a sound wave.

wavelength – One complete cycle of a waveform.

white noise – A noise used for testing and calibration that is comprised of all frequencies. Sounds like that static noise when you're between stations on a radio.

woofer – A speaker designed to reproduce low (bass) frequencies.

XLR – A three-pin connector used for microphones and pro audio equipment.

About the Author

Lonnie Park has seen the music business from many perspectives, his experience spanning from music performance to sound-system design and consulting. His education began in a Christian school in central New York. As a communications major in college, he studied audio and recording while performing in various music venues. At age seventeen, he toured the U.S. as a sound engineer on a tour for Christian Contemporary artists. As a sound engineer and musician, he worked on both ends of various sound systems and studios. This exposure helped to provide an expanded understanding of the diversity in worship styles and their subsequent needs.

At the age of twenty-three, Mr. Park and a partner opened Ultimate Music, a recording studio and retail business that sells and services a broad range of musical instruments and sound systems. Designing systems for the many churches that had become regular customers, he developed a unique approach to "Churches, not just buildings, in need of sound systems."

As a recording engineer, musician, and vocalist, and songwriter, Mr. Park has appeared on a wide range of recordings. Both religious and secular, his credits range from regional projects to worldwide releases. He continues to be an integral part of Ultimate Music, based in Cortland, New York, and remains active in the music business.

Lonnie Park
c/o Ultimate Music
884 Route 13
Cortland, NY 13045
(607)756-5456

email: lonnie@ultimatemusiccenter.com

Basic System Layout

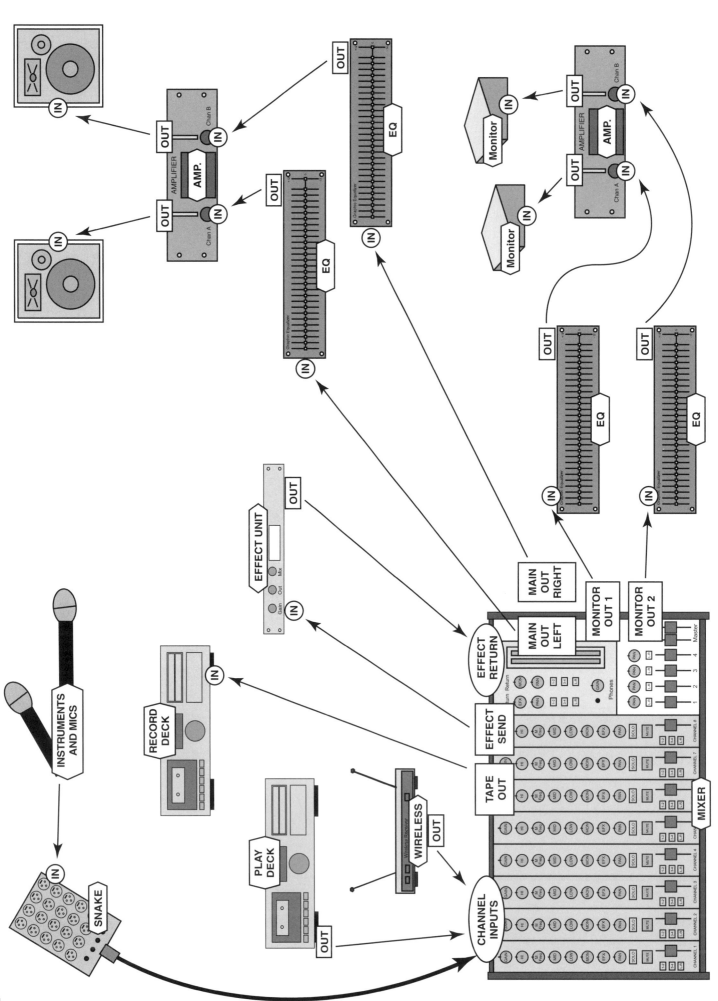

Biamped System Layout

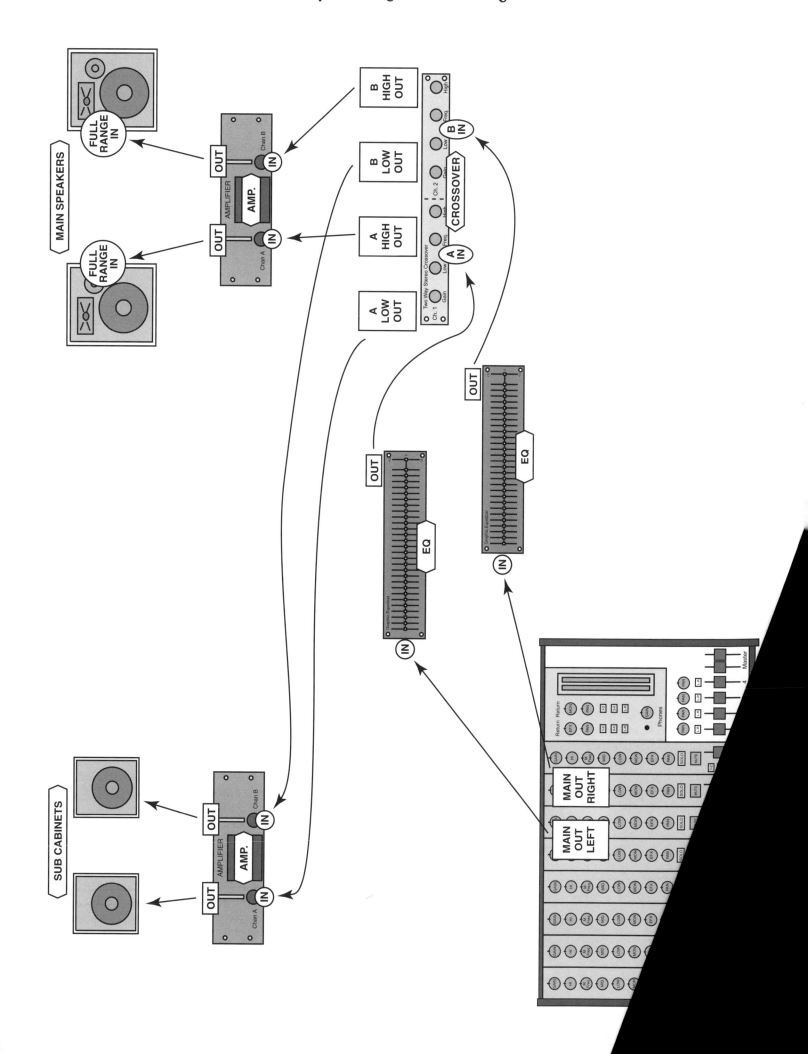

AUDIO TECHNOLOGY BOOKS

FROM HAL LEONARD

Mackie Compact Mixers – 2nd Edition

Now in its expanded and updated second edition, Mackie Compact Mixers takes the mystery out of using your mixer. Written in a clear, musician-friendly style, this book will help you get the most from your small mixer, whatever its brand or model. Provides specific information and hook-up examples on Mackie's most popular models, including the "classic" 1202 and 1604 as well as the new 1202-, 1402-, 1604-VLZs, VLZ Pro and other models. Written by the author of Live Sound for Musicians and authorized by Mackie, this book explains the fundamental concepts of how mixing boards work, emphasizing how audio gets into and out of a mixer. Armed with this understanding of signal flow, you will be equipped to begin answering your own questions about how to set up and operate your mixer to best meet your needs.

00330477..$27.95

The Recording Guitarist

A Guide for Home and Studio by Jon Chappell

This is a practical, hands-on guide to a variety of recording environments, from modest home studios – where the guitarist must also act as the engineer and producer – to professional facilities outfitted with top-quality gear and staffed with audio engineers. This book will prepare guitarists for any recording situation and will help them become familiar with all facets of recording technology and procedure. Topics covered include: guitars and amps for recording; effects; mixer logic and routing strategies; synching music to moving images; and how to look and sound professional, with advice from Alex Lifeson, Carl Verheyen, Steve Lukather, Eric Johnson and others. Also includes complete info on the classic set-ups of 14 guitar greats, from Hendrix to Vai.

00330335..$19.95

Audio Made Easy – 2nd Edition

Audio Made Easy is a book about professional audio written in terms that everyone can understand. Chapters include info on mixers, microphones, amplifiers, speakers and how they all work together. New edition features a new section on wireless mics. New edition features a new section on wireless mics.

....$12.95

Yamaha Guide to Sound Systems for Worship

The Yamaha Guide to Sound Systems for Worship is written to assist in the design, purchase, and operation of a sound system. It provides the basic information on sound systems that is most needed by ministers, members of Boards of Trustees and worship and music committees, interested members of congregations, and even employees of musical instrument dealers that sell sound systems. To be of greatest value to all, it is written to be both nondenominational and "non-brand-name."

00290243..$24.95

Live Sound for Musicians

Finally, a live sound book written for musicians, not engineers! Live Sound for Musicians tells you everything you need to know to keep your band's PA system working smoothly, from set-up to sound check right through performance. Author Rudy Trubitt give you all the information you need, and leaves out the unnecessary propeller-head details that would just slow you down. So if you're the player in the band who sets up the PA, this is the book you've been waiting for!

00330249..$19.95

Sound Check – The Basics of Sound and Sound Systems

Sound Check is a simplified guide to what can be a tricky subject: getting good sound. Starting with an easy-to-understand explanation of the principles and physics of sound, Sound Check goes on to cover amplifiers, speaker hookup, matching speakers with amps, sound reinforcement, mixers, monitor systems, grounding, and more.

00330118..$14.95

Yamaha Sound Reinforcement Handbook – 2nd Edition

Sound reinforcement is the use of audio amplification systems. This book is the first and only book of its kind to cover all aspects of designing and using such systems for public address and musical performance. The book features information on both the audio theory involved and the practical applications of that theory, explaining everything from microphones to loud speakers. This revised edition features almost 40 new pages and is even easier to follow with the addition of an index and a simplified page and chapter numbering system. New topics covered include: MIDI, synchronization, and an appendix on logarithms.

00500964..$34.95